Lun[ch at the]
Elephant & Castle

Katrina Naomi

Templar Poetry

First Published 2008 by Templar Poetry
Templar Poetry is an imprint of Delamide & Bell

Fenelon House,
Kingsbridge Terrace
58 Dale Road, Matlock, Derbyshire
DE4 3NB

www.templarpoetry.co.uk

ISBN 978-1-906285-24-1

A CIP catalogue record for this book is available from the British Library

Typeset by Pliny
Graphics by Paloma Violet
Printed and bound in Turkey

for Tim and Melissa

Acknowledgements

Thanks are due to the editors of the following, in which versions of some of these poems first appeared: *Coffee House Poetry; goldfish; Ink, Sweat and Tears; Magma; Mint Sauce* (Cinnamon Press); *Orbis; Piqué* (Templar Poetry) and *Solitaire* (Templar Poetry); also to Resonance FM for broadcasting several of these poems.

Thanks to all tutors, staff and friends at Goldsmiths, particularly to my tutors Maura Dooley and Eva Salzman. I would also like to thank: Andy, Barry, Chrissie, Emma, Gemma, Judy, Magda, Maria, Mary, Melissa, Mick, Nan, Ruth, Sarah and Tim.

Finally, thanks to the Arvon Foundation for a grant, and thanks to the organisers, tutors and poets of the Jerwood Aldeburgh Seminar 2008.

ARTS COUNCIL ENGLAND

Contents

Tunnel of Love

It looked uncertain.
I tottered in, heels
skittering on the pink plastic.
There were water trails
before the pleasure boat rocked.
My rocker was on board.

I say 'my', he was anyone's,
with his bleached blond quiff,
curl caressing his left eyebrow,
scar bisecting the right,
so he looked almost symmetrical,
apart from his hands.

His hands were all over me,
before we'd even sat
on the wet, moulded seats.
And I never did. I sat on his lap.
My neat, white pencil skirt,
tight as a condom.

He couldn't pull it up or down.
It wrinkled along my untouched body,
wedged against his heaving drainpipes.

Yet we bobbed, as one,
bashed into the fake grass
and the fibre glass cave, together.

I had so little for him to squeeze,
as we juddered through the darkness.
His hormones masked by Brut,
£1.99 from the precinct,
and that gorgeous roll-up,
which tasted all the better on his tongue.

He called it his 'shag break',
his other recreation,
aside from riding the dodgems,
leaping from one to another
with balletic ease in his narrow jeans,
like a sexy bus conductor.

And he was thin, tight muscles
alert in his black t-shirt,
little more than a boy.
Yet he looked so much older,
cruising the dodgems with his sneer,
chipped tooth and chiselled hair.

I knew enough to keep my hands
out of his hair. I kissed him hard,
slid off his lap in the sunshine.
He didn't help me out of the boat,
just lit another cigarette, its tip
sparking the way to the electric cars.

Flight

Elizabeth Bishop sits open on my lap.
I've a head full of icebergs (imagined)
and Newfoundland (real),
as I wake mid-air in this baby blue scene,
gazing down from a mountain (imagined).
Should the engine cut (imagined),
I'll fall (real) into that messy icing,
serene one side, glacial the other (imagined),
carry on through to those whales of cloud,
scarring the shallows off the coast.

Another Planet

She's leaving this planet,
her roses neglected for spanners, bolts.
I hadn't read the signs, didn't know
she'd been working on that rocket.
And it's complete. I can't think
why I didn't see it before. I see now
she's packed a small leather case.
So few items. I know so little
about this new earth, if there's a moon,
a sun, lakes, a tide. She's changing
into her silk dress and jacket,
plumping her hair. She doesn't look back
as she shoulders into her coat.
The kitchen door hovers in the artificial breeze.
She's left me everything.

Tulips

Raised far away,
this one wears sheaths
of sherbert lemon,
soft and yielding.

These beauties will swell,
unfurling to show
what they've got, forcing
their virginal sisters

out of the light.
Already my hands are damp
for you. Don't be shy,
I've chosen you.

You all go the same way:
Look at me. And I do.
You're mine till I tire of you,
or your bloom fades.

I've put you in the window,
now work for me.

Sound and Vision

The cement mixer
       turns
like a workman's
       thoughts,
over and over,
       squeaks regularly,
afternoon sex
       on a Spanish bed.
Then shudders.

The workmen
       stop
their shovelling
       when I walk
up the street,
       stare.
The jut
       of their chins
says it all.

Door safely shut,
       I rock
in my seat.
       Wish
one of those
       workmen
was better looking.

Walking Away from People, Lights, Tracks

I stay on the train.
It jolts forward, almost empty,
I follow, head almost empty.

I carry on north, north, north.

London drifts on through towns
that have lost all identity.
I watch two girls pretend Milton Keynes is Brixton.

Then it's green - willows, dog walkers, rivers.

I empty my briefcase out of the window.
I have nothing, except these clothes
and £41.37.

Left it - overdue library books, rare Coltrane vinyl,
festering poems, National Film Theatre membership,
flat, wife, job.

Over the border in a smallish town,
beginning to walk
away from people, lights, tracks.

All that's real are the stones and leaves
under my feet, the swishing air
of each step away.

From now on it's bins, berries, streams.
Tonight, I do well, an empty holiday let.
Tomorrow, moving on.

A month goes by.
Nobody notices a man of middle age
with a warmer coat and a new moustache.

Just don't look into my eyes, which are burning blue.

The Slow Train

The red ink skated on the script, after that call. I was aware only of a low sound made by some animal near my desk, and people gathering, my boss looking at me. Through mountains of air, I was talking, explaining in a voice that wasn't mine. My boss held me, which I knew went against our workplace's code of conduct, but how good her touch felt.

I went to stand and the carpet squares surfed in sequence. Mary walked me to the tube. The ticket barrier was all arms and legs. Mary had her hand, awkward, on my arm, from Brixton to Victoria. She bought us both brandies, and saw me onto the Margate train. I cried solidly. Only one man glanced at me. I was an actor in a film he'd seen before.

I went straight to her. She reached for me from the sheet's constraints. She spoke my name. It took four years.

The Night Club

The man in drag is Jordanesque.
Breasts scaffolded, squashed into silver
sequins. Long, black beehived hair,
three-inch heels, two-inch lashes,
lips pearled a palest pink. Turns
out to be a woman when she sings.

Everyone smokes, drinks imported whisky,
a glass the price of a week's wage.
I'm the only foreigner. The music hypnotic,
but no one's dancing. Men
in sharp, cream-jacketed suits,
crocodile shoes, mouth Addis hits.

I taste my beer, smiling in the darkness.
The singer slinks to the bar.
Two men move in. She
lights her own cigarette. She's shorter
than I thought, legs chunky, arms
thick, earrings like barrel-hoops.

She blows a double 'O' in my direction,
then twists to show her low-cut back.
She'll be singing tonight,
still writhing in that scanty shift. And
I think of her, if I think of Ethiopia,
which is not so often. Not really.

11

My Fathers

One wore a St Christopher, the other a watch,
one liked cricket, the other football,
one drove a Lotus, the other a Morris,
one was a nurse, the other sold turf,
one read Orwell, the other The Sun,
one sported a tweed jacket, the other leather,
one listened to brass bands, the other to Brubeck,
one took me to Brands Hatch, the other to Butlins,
one was Catholic, the other C of E,
one drank bitter, the other whisky,
one was Clairol's 'Natural Nordic', the other a darker blond,
one hit my mother, the other hit my dog.
I haven't seen either of them in years.

The Håmeflost Mittens

At the ceremony,
all the village of Håmeflost gathered.
Every young girl's hair
washed and plaited
under winter hats.

The village leader
with strong, guttural voice,
presented my first pair of mittens.
Long before the great snowfall,
I loved their rich, mottled skin.

I can still push my fingers wide
into the yellowy-white of the inner fur:
these mittens of seal skin,
polar bear fleece. Unfashionable.
But that's how it is, for us. Or was.

Like two battered beaver wings,
the mittens sag on the back
of the bedroom door,
dark, against the pine
of my bright, bland, urban flat.

My city friends criticise. A part
of me wishes the mittens weren't fur,
but they are. Some nights, I sing
to the seal, sing to the polar bear.
We all did.

I don't tell my city friends this,
or of the call of the north.

Miss LaLa

(after Degas)

I saw the painting by accident.
No room for accidents in my game.
I'm not one for exhibitions,
makes my head spin, all those colours,
but a gentleman friend told me.
It was above even his price range,
I couldn't credit it.
He took me to the gallery.
Of course, I dressed respectable,
bonnet and gloves.
No one could tell the resemblance,
if resemblance there was,
my legs fatter, my hair a shock.
Odd to see myself as others do,
hanging from the ceiling by a cord.

Fightback

I'd always suspected it would happen,
sometime. I was 17, when it did.

I was cycling back south from Carnival,
when he rammed his racing bike into mine.

He was white. Blond spiked hair, good looking, cute,
before he hit me in the face and ribs,

knocked me off the saddle to the pavement.
I wouldn't ever want it like this, his

ferocious tearing at my clothes, forcing
my shirt up to my neck, mauling my pecs,

busting the buttons of my flies, grabbing
my balls, pulling my hair, yanking the back

of my jeans down, down. I fought him as best
I could, bit into his white skin real hard.

He hit me again. Then stopped. Climbed off me.
Spat: *You're not fucking worth it anyway.*

I've set out to prove just how wrong he was.

The Osteopath

On our first date,
we dance,
my hand at her waist,

or rather she dances,
lonely steps,
rocking from foot

to foot. While I lie
on the couch, arm outstretched,
her hands flamenco

my clavicle,
reaching their duende
to her clean white tempo.

B Movie

You have to be blonde
or jet black, either way, sister
there's a lot of dyeing.

You have to forget what you see,
remember aliases,
but don't get smart.

You'll get used to the eyes
of the rest of the mob,
they'll go no further.

You'll smoke at all hours:
first thing in your silk camisole,
4 am in your fox fur.

You spend days alone,
turning his diamonds in your palm,
arranging imaginary flights to Rio.

You spend nights waiting,
ready by the phone,
pistol out of the bedside drawer.

You know there's a wife, Italian,
that he's got children
and you won't have any of your own.

You know you'll live
in a series of apartments,
each less elaborate than the last.

Learning to Love Beer

Squatting in the corner of Nan and Pa's lounge,
demijohns of fuggles and goldings, fizzing,
fermenting, in their filthy oceans of yeast,
stoppered with a regiment of pink rubber bungs.

And one morning, coming downstairs to the sick
of an explosion up the cream wall, over the swirled carpet,
the patterned curtain, patterned again with a brown film
of nearly-beer, which was too potent for this life.

Pa grumbled at the waste, the expense of it,
the glass jar surprised to find itself in two parts.
Nan stood amid the mess, arms folded over her housecoat:
the days of brewing in the garden shed were here.

I'd help skim the residue, rack the old, rouse the new.
There were trips to Margate for Boots' Home Brew Kit
and more demijohns of thicker glass, making my hands
lose their blood, white-green against their moulded hips.

We'd crouch next to slug pellets and rusting propellers,
tear packets, add water, sugar, malt, and breathe deep.
Nothing was measured. Chief Taster from an early age, I grew
a liking for bitter, could tell its sweetness, when it was off.

With a dodgy heater, we'd work in the cold of autumn
so there was beer for winter. I'd only drink in the shed with Pa,
at first, the froth lining his clipped naval moustache,
the scummed tide bursting on the bridge of my nose.

Lunch at the Elephant & Castle

I hadn't thought of you, hadn't thought of
you walking into The George, but you did.

And through the smoke and people standing up,
you saw me lying on the carpet with

Andy, was that his name? I'm not too sure.
I do remember how much I'd fancied

him. He was blond, while you're dark, blue-eyed while
yours are grey. I don't think you've forgotten

have you? I don't have much of an excuse,
except it was lunchtime and I hadn't

eaten, but I had drunk nine bottles of
Becks, so lying at the back of The George

with, let's call him, Andy seemed OK.
Perhaps it was, until I was aware

of your leopard print shoes next to my head,
and the way you said nothing. I'm grateful

for that. You put out your hand, helped me to
my feet and walked me back to Lambeth North.

It was then that I knew I wanted you.

Elegy

It was a public death.
Well, we were all there
but only my sister and I
were awake for it.

We watched in awe:
like at the birth of puppies,
like at the firing of a human cannon,
like something we'd never seen.

And the peace after
that last outlandish breath.
We sat savouring it.
I looked at my sister -

Do you think? She did.
It's what we'd been waiting for,
for the four days we'd been
camped around her bed.

It was like an outing:
chips or curry brought in at night,
a bottle of sherry during the day -
but at 3.50 am, it was over.

I walked to a corridor for a nurse.
There was no rush,
I found I went slowly, feeling
my socks against the polished floor.

The nurse felt and looked.
Yes.
And mum just lay there
through it all.

Picnic

Here you are
with your vintage hamper
that scrapes my legs,
your posh sandwiches,
your white wine, chilled,
and I wonder if it'll work,
this day with its promise
of sex and a lazy river,
if the chardonnay
will do its job,
or have us argue,
sat at opposite ends
of the tartan rug,
crushing daisies.

Birdsongs are Composed of Love Notes and Pleasure Notes

There's no dictionary, so I sit with a tape recorder and note-book, pressing buttons, listening and writing. I've learnt basic Pheasant. Blackbird and Robin I'm struggling with.

I don't have the right-shaped beak and my throat is too large. There's a robin who sits by me. I can't understand if it's love, and I'm worried. How would we kiss?

I imagine he'd be good with his wings. I can feel the rub of his little chest. But I can't give him any more, not yet, just the slightest of caresses. I haven't the words.

The Avenue at Middelharnis

(after Hobbema)

Strange trees en route.
        They are spindly, taller
than seems possible
        for such trunks.
They'd snap in any wind,
        which must arrive
in so flat and endless
        a land. The man
with the pipe
        and frock coat
tending his trees
        (smaller versions
of the same) does not
        return my greeting.
I walk past
        another man,
glued to a flute,
        and his dog, mid-
sniff. It doesn't bark,
        doesn't wag its tail.
I hear a note
        from the flute,

high-pitched,
  continuous,
has been playing
  for decades, as if
disaster has befallen
  this place. That couple
over there won't love,
  won't argue, but
maintain a fixed
  distance apart,
near shorter,
  more realistic trees.
The only birds
  are stuck to a cloud.
If I carry on,
  I'll arrive
at the frozen town,
  with its steeple,
its market square.
  Is this immortality?

Blood Atlas

A whole geography of blood.
I spend years of my life bleeding,
staining the sheets while I dock
at the small map of Sri Lanka,
waking at the Isle of Wight.

These darkening reds of destination,
journeys I've always shunned.
A show of what might have been,
somewhere I've yet to berth -
a place I don't want to go.

An Everyday Story of Mortgages

I come across the fields,
with map, compass and torch,
warm in my balaclava and gloves.

I climb the last stile
and cross the lane
then onto the track

to the potter's house.
The lights are out,
there's no moon.

She lives alone.
It's extremely easy
and you've paid me well.

I work the lock,
a click, then silence.
I'm in.

Her bedroom's round the back,
near her studio.
I hear her light snore.

I don't actually enjoy this bit,
though I suppose people think I do
but it's lucrative.

The pillow is down.
She's old.
I barely sweat.

She looks peaceful.
A few months later,
you buy the house.

Of course, the price came down,
others put off
by the circumstances.

You move in, as planned.
Your pottery thrives.
It's a beautiful house.

I come across the fields.